JAZZ PIANO SOLOS   VOLUME 6   SECOND EDITION

# hard bop

Arranged by Brent Edstrom

ISBN 978-1-5400-7143-9

Visit Hal Leonard Online at
**www.halleonard.com**

Contact us:
**Hal Leonard**
7777 West Bluemound Road
Milwaukee, WI 53213
Email: info@halleonard.com

In Europe, contact:
**Hal Leonard Europe Limited**
42 Wigmore Street
Marylebone, London, W1U 2RN
Email: info@halleonardeurope.com

In Australia, contact:
**Hal Leonard Australia Pty. Ltd.**
4 Lentara Court
Cheltenham, Victoria, 3192 Australia
Email: info@halleonard.com.au

# contents

# AIREGIN

By SONNY ROLLINS

**Fast Swing**

To Coda ⊕

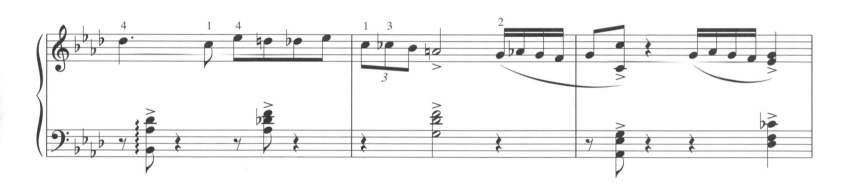

D.C. al Coda

CODA

# BLUES MARCH

By BENNY GOLSON

**Moderate Blues Shuffle**

**To Coda** ⊕

**D.S. al Coda**

**CODA**

*rit.*

# BLUE SOUL

By BLUE MITCHELL

**To Coda**

# CANTELOPE ISLAND

By HERBIE HANCOCK

**Medium Jazz Funk**

*Solo based on one by Herbie Hancock*

D.S. al Coda

CODA

Repeat and Fade

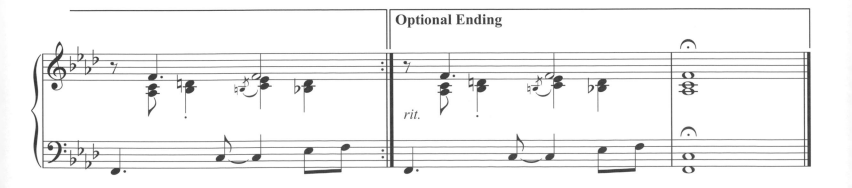

Optional Ending

# CEORA

By LEE MORGAN

**Moderate Bossa Nova**

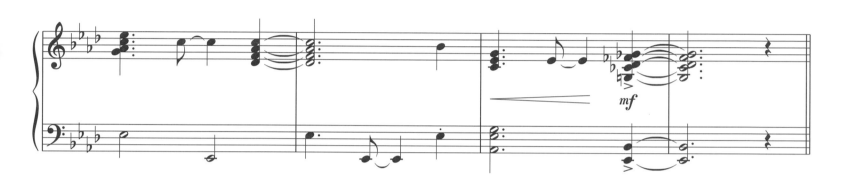

# THE CHAMP

By DIZZY GILLESPIE

**Fast Swing**

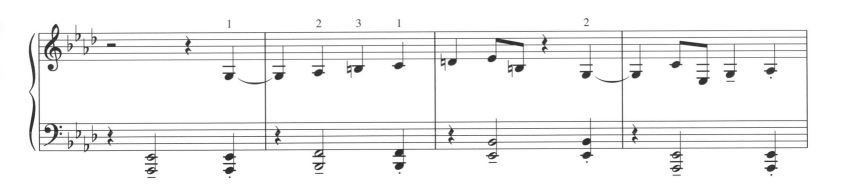

# EMANCIPATION BLUES

By OLIVER NELSON

# GIANT STEPS

By JOHN COLTRANE

To Coda

44

D.C. al Coda

CODA

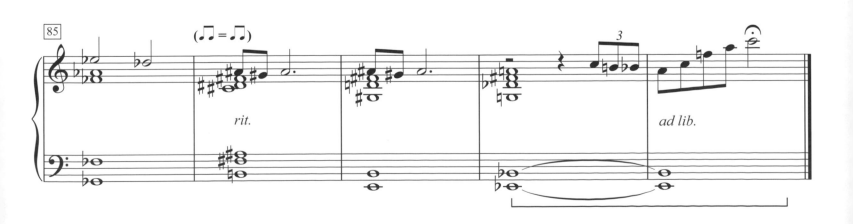

# I REMEMBER CLIFFORD

By BENNY GOLSON

# I REMEMBER BIRD

By LEONARD FEATHER

**Slow Blues feel**

D.S. al Coda

**CODA**

*rit.*

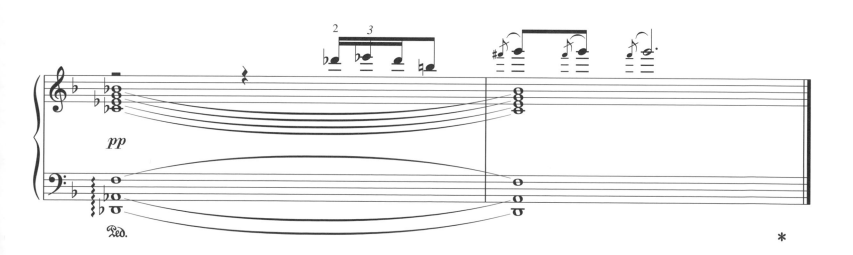

*pp*

# THE JIVE SAMBA

By NAT ADDERLEY

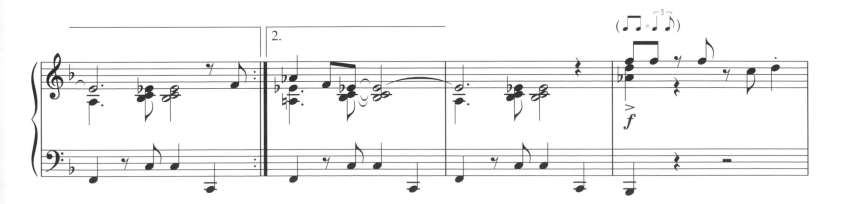

**D.C. al Coda**

# MERCY, MERCY, MERCY

By JOSEF ZAWINUL

**Slow Funky Rock**

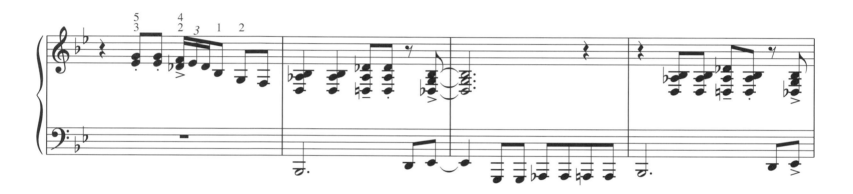

# NICA'S DREAM

Words and Music by
HORACE SILVER

**Moderately fast Latin**

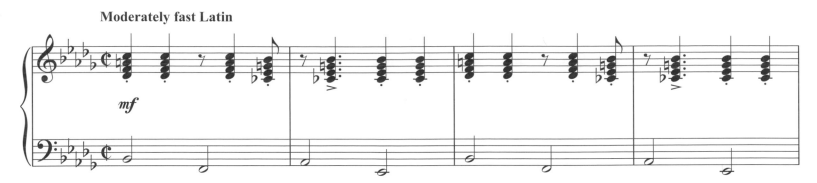

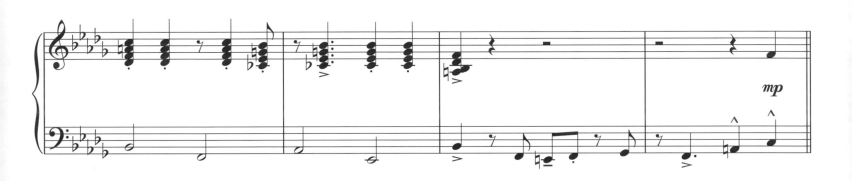

# SIDEWINDER

By LEE MORGAN

**Moderately slow Funk**

# SONG FOR MY FATHER

Words and Music by
HORACE SILVER

**Bossa Nova**

**Swing 8ths (March feel)**
*right hand over left hand*

# TOUR DE FORCE

By JOHN "DIZZY" GILLESPIE

**Medium Swing**

# THIS HERE

By BOBBY TIMMONS

**Medium Gospel feel**

# WORK SONG

By NAT ADDERLEY

**Bright Swing**

To Coda ⊕

*8vb throughout*

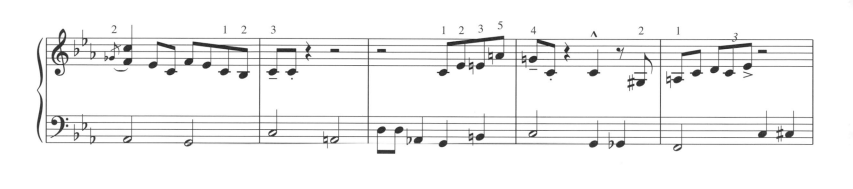